Pretty, Rooster

Clay Matthews

Cooper
Dillon

Cooper Dillon Books
San Diego, California
CooperDillon.com

"Domasticate" comic by Shannon Wheeler
"Shaving" comic by Micah Farritor
The cover features a sculpture in wire by Spencer Little
Cover photograph by Misha M. Johnson
Cover Design, flipbook, & section breaks by Max Xiantu

ISBN-10: 0-9841928-4-0
ISBN-13: 978-0-9841928-4-7

Printed in the United States

Acknowledgments:

Grateful acknowledgment is made to the editors and staff
of the following publications, in which some of these poems
first appeared:

Anti- : "Mental Aerobics"
Burnside Review : "Railroad Sonnet"
Puerto del Sol : "Break/fast", "Pickup"
Spinning Jenny : "Market"
Still : "Vine", "Leash", "Potting Soil"

Lastly, endless thanks to my teachers, friends, and family.

CONTENTS

COCKSCOMB THE FIRST

COCKSCOMB THE SECOND

COCKSCOMB THE THIRD

Pretty, Rooster

Clay Matthews

Domasticate

Clay Matthews

Shannon Wheele[r]

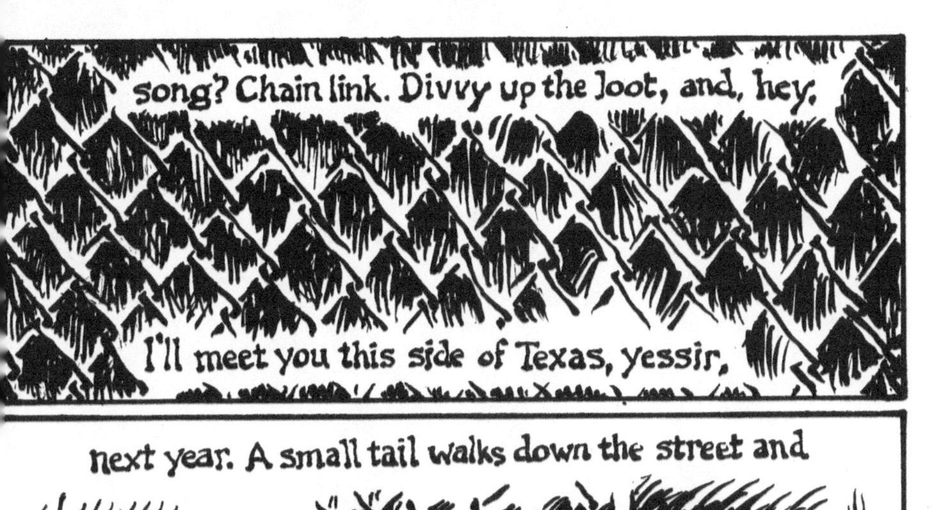
song? Chain link. Divvy up the loot, and, hey.
I'll meet you this side of Texas, yessir,

next year. A small tail walks down the street and
everything goes crazy. The wind, the loud

thunder that split my dream last night, and ran
me ragged in two directions. I howled

in one. In the other, I walked the black
road. Fences everywhere. Then I came back.

for Jan

I had a rooster, my rooster pleased me,
I fed my rooster 'neath the greenberry tree.
My little rooster went, Cock-a-doo-dle doo,
Dee doo-dle-ee, doo-dle-ee, doodle-ee do.

—"I Had a Rooster," Traditional

Bulbous

Daffodils. Too many syllables to
start but we start and our hearts start breathing
the morning fog, dove, coffee, and don't you
tell me I look tired, I know I do. Sing,
brother. Sister, put your panties in the
drawer. Spring comes on like jealousy, green
and mean and growing all over in a
small round pot beside the soda machine
outside the liquor store. I thirst. It rains.
The sun comes up over mountain. Begin
family, begin the ducks, the slow pain
of biting necks, quick sex, a good, wet sin.
Slowly I rise from bed. Slowly I look
out glass, guilty now, unshaven, a crook.

Resignation

The azaleas go up and out like fire
-works. Birds sing. If you put your hand right now
on the ground, you would feel it beating. Wire
runs around the neighbors' fence, pulsing low
electric thuds to keep the dog in. Planes
fly over, animals look up, fall back
into their naps, and on a porch the names
of women roll around two men's mouths, slack
from beer as they crack another, the can
crisp. Hey, it's springtime. And why not? We have
all been patient. We've all behaved. Sun, then
clouds. Night, then day. We get around. We wave
to each other out walking. The dogs smell
other dogs. Dusk comes, and it's just as well.

Wings

Mowers run and I look up at the moon
in the mid-day sky, white and pale, spectre
-thin, says Keats. I kind of feel that the room
closes around me. I kind of feel her
behind me, saying I think right now that
I want to hold a baby. Shadows grow
long in the morning, short mid-day and at
dusk they cut right through me. The branches know
their reach, their thousand fingers cast upon
the bedroom wall. We roll all over each
other. The paint wears in places. I'm done
asking the moon for answers. I beseech
nothing from the half-cast face. When she walks
through the room I hear her hips' slow white talk.

Underdog

Saturday and NASCAR down the road in
Bristol. I wax my truck, turn the motor
over and inspect the belts. An engine
is a hard thing to understand. Never
said I was fast. And never said I was
easy. Planes fly over with banner ads.
I want to buy things but I don't because
I'm broke. I don't know what I want. What fads
I have seen come and go. What days, races.
The television at the little bar
goes back and forth, cars running, then paces
to March college basketball games. We wait
for a Cinderalla story. You know
how it goes. Have a beer. Enjoy the show.

Breakfast

The neighbor's roosters crow all day. Sometimes
it becomes comical the way the world
keeps spinning around. I wake up and sign
checks for the bills. I drink coffee. I hurl
my hopes and fears into the abyss. So,
I don't remember if you said we would
get groceries today. So, I don't know
how chickens have sex. But it seems I should,
being one who eats the eggs, being one
who listens to their song in the distance.
It is not music. It is music. Gone
on along the black road, a cry, a trance
for whatever it is we cry out for
at dawn, dusk, always, on the yard's small shore.

Leash

Cold streets and a cigarette. I have found
I return to certain things. The mornings,
for instance. A desire for streetlights wound
up in a larger desire for big things
to happen. And the radio preacher
says Through great God big things can happen! But
I don't know about god, only weather,
lightning, the sound of wind shaking trees shut.
I open, and they seem to speak through their
leaves. We all go away, and that is a
hard thing to deal with. I look out to where
the people walk the roads, with dogs, with the
promise of everlasting life, tin cans,
children, mail boxes, thinking: it happens.

Mental Aerobics

The morning paper, and my neck is fucked
from sleeping wrong. I can't get this crossword
right. 29 Down: _____________ of the old blanked
blankety-blank. Late last night the stars heard
this rumor from this planet about how
things would shake down today. It goes like this:
If you want change, there is no time like now.
I don't know what I want. Some eggs. A kiss
from the woman in the other room. Health.
I am sick. Not well. But it is spring and
so thank you for the flowers. A word with
four letters, beginning with "L." A wand
I can wave around to make the answers
appear: last. Lost. Long. Love—yeah, that one, sure.

Pick-Up

South-side of town and I drive in for some
pizza, beers to go. They do the dirty
eats right on this end. I don't know what home
means, exactly. I take it at thirty
to mean people, place, real things, some good food.
Good and home being relative. Also
relative, being relative. The dude
in the booth with bad teeth wants me to know
he's been moving, washers and dryers, big
stuff mostly. It's good sometimes to see that
people are getting on with their lives, dig,
that they're out there living, wading through what
must sometimes feel like home to them, or must
always, cheese and crust, windows, floors, and dust.

Sonnet with a Little Mustard on It

On this date in 1941, Bob
Feller threw the only no-hitter on
opening day, ever. I am a blob
of insignificance this morning, gone
from the minds of everyone, right now. Right
now I don't really care about baseball,
nor history, nor Bob Feller, but light
begins a day well, and pitching can stall
the inevitable. That being? Death?
0-1, or 1-0, or better
sex with the Missus that night, Bob, is wealth
measured in gold, or touch, or long letters
from fans saying, Bob, we love you? I think
of the day and swing, as the white ball sinks.

Break/Fast

We are mostly quiet. I don't scream much
at anything. The lawnmower, perhaps.
A light snow, early April, it is such
a sad story, every time the tree saps
itself back up. No sugar this morning.
But you're sweet. Sometimes, early, when the sun
just bends around the gray clouds, I see wings
in the asphalt puddles, I mistake one
blackbird for one starling, one starling for
another. Some of them eat the grass seed
I've put down. I am not bothered, no, nor
frightened, today. I wash myself. I feed
myself. The white plate shines. The birds dip down
and eat the wet things rising from the ground.

Analog

I turn on some old beat records and call
for a little more bourbon. Some nights we
dance in the small spaces between the wall,
the couch, the future. The moon is a she,
right now. I read an article that said
a bit of booze is good for you. Then I
read another that said not. Then I read
of a sociological study
that proved romantic love, under the right
circumstances, could endure. I wonder
what's right. The music, for instance. The light
of the small lamp glowing in the corner.
If you want a couplet, look no further
than this. If you want a song, listen here.

Cockscomb the First

At the Old School

April 21 and the wild flower
seeds still sit in the basement. Yesterday
kids across the country gave up power
and got high nonstop. Things are in the way
between here and the path to the sublime.
Sun and rain and days, for instance. When will
I die? A seed sprouted hangs on just fine
with the little it has to hang on. Still,
not everybody makes it all the time.
In fact, no one, but it's 8:05 now
and I am alive, I breathe and I climb
through the next day, blooms and a white dress, how
did I get here, and how good to be here,
the buses squeal and I am everywhere.

Loch Ness

28

The buses squeal and I am everywhere.
Half past Alabama, quarter past eight.
A marriage, and there's some boxed things down there
in the basement I'd like to lose. Like hate,
envy, greed, all the bad things but then all
the bad things are only bad given bad
-ness. I read a book on monsters once. Y'all
don't know what it was like to be all clad
in darkness, scared of the dark. The lil' dog
sleeps. I am awake, and in the other
room she turns into blossoms, takes a long
float for a while. Here we miss our mothers.
It is impossible not to. It is
and it is impossible not to wish.

Sweetwater, TN

And it is impossible not to wish
for all these dreams I keep in the little
side chamber of my heart. We watched the fish
swim in a lake buried in the riddle
of a cave. I-75, the lost sea
they stocked with rainbow trout, and the big man
in front of the boat asking our lady
How soon until they're blind? How quickly can
they fail to see? In the darkness, blindness
comes like a setting sun, the color fades
so what was once rainbow is now just bless-
éd trout, finned myth, fed down here in Hades
for the tourists, like us. They throw them food.
They shine the light and they scatter for good.

Neighborhood Watch

They shine the light and they scatter for good,
the skateboarders across the lot, smoking,
the senior citizen's center. They've food
and dancing to music inside. They sing
the old songs. There is a place for all
of us. The man with thick glasses asked me
if I believed in god by the north wall
and I thought of a tree I once climbed. Trees
being perhaps evidence of god, I
thought of a hundred ways to answer him,
but said nothing. Outside the cops roll by
now. I am older but they still frighten
me. So much frightens me. I am afraid.
I'm scared of the sirens. Then the night fades.

Death Letter

I'm scared of the sirens. Then the night fades.
In the morning the neighbor's dogs shit on
our lawn. The grass comes up, it is Tuesday.
Bob Dylan says, The place was really an
asylum with no spiritual hope of
any kind. You love people. And when they
ask you to bring cigarettes, out of love
you do even though they're dying. What say
we get out of this place. I am afraid
of hospitals. 9:09 A.M. and
I wonder what you are doing. All grayed
and older. All blonde and young. We're not sand,
we are eternal. We're not eternal,
we're dust. Then wind blows and we buckle.

Vows

32

We're dust. Then wind blows and we buckle
the latches. We shut the doors. Storm season
and the flowers bend over. My uncle
used to drink too much and then lose reason
and sleep in the garden. The seeds still sit
in the basement. We're going to grow some
flowers for our wedding day. You get white
and I get cold beer. We'll bend around it
like vine. Pronouns escape me but I fill
them up like planters. I'mma blossom, soon,
babe. I'm gonna bloom. We are what we will
to be, and we'll be what we can. The moon
is just a sliver now, scratching the sky.
Come June I'm gonna look you in the eye.

Christened

Come June I'm gonna look you in the eye.
The moon, the woman in lace. It's your face
that keeps turning. April 28, my
hands a calendar of carnal embrace.
When will I die? Seeds in paper, seeds in
the ground, seeds fallen dead from the tree, now
wet, now green. Now no questions, now we swim
in the cold water. No ox now, no plow.
Have I ever told you you're beautiful?
I am alive. I scatter all over
the earth. In the lake, in the metal hull
of a boat in a cave, they set sail, there
in the darkness, there with a little light,
there still with color left, there still with sight.

Talking Dirty

34

Kids on the trampoline at the trailer
park, and behind everything a well-tilled
garden. I respect things like this, older,
and I think it takes a long time and filled
with toil to really know a machine. So,
I've learned to be sweet to the mower, and
a little bit rough with two-strokes. You know,
I saw on the news some people have grand
affairs with objects—one woman even
took as her last name Eiffel, having had
a ceremony with the tower. When
everything makes sense, I'll stop talking. Said:
come on now, motor, you sweet machine, give
us a little start, get going babe: live.

Consumed

Hwy 11 flea market and men
walk the aisles with the guns they have just bought.
The women look at purses. And I am
stereotyping the genders. I've got
eyes, though. This is what I see. A little
Mexican vendor, warm tortillas, pork
-skin tacos, fresh cilantro, we whittle
the day into meals with a knife and fork.
There's too much to look at, too many hands
busy with something, too many random
tools and gadgets and teeth biting gold bands.
We eat a bag of candied pecans, some
still warm. The pickles, fries. America,
I walk with you, as you point: this, that, the.

Practice

Tuesday and all I can think is that I'd
like a shot of tequila. A small bird
dips its head in the gutter, opens wide
its wings and I lay down and afterward
hold a pillow. Kids just down the street play
ball in the afternoons, and some late nights
I sit in the driveway and take up gray
gravel, throw it into the air, swing right
through whatever bothers me into what
feels solid in sending a rock out deep
into a field. Maybe I just can't shut
out the darkness. Maybe I shouldn't keep
dreaming so hard. I am too old to want
so much. I'm too young to believe I can't.

Potting Soil

Mid-week and we plant flowers. Not flowers,
but seeds. I can't ever really decide
if there's a difference. Is there a space, there,
between the sun and rain, the clouds that hide
the cosmos of a thousand beautiful
things behind them? Two bucks at the check-out
line, a bit of dirt, water, and boom: you
have made something worth making. I could shout
for love if that were the right thing to do.
Frost fades away. The asphalt takes on its
edges the grass like a child on the new
hem of a woman's dress. I say, please, let's
not forget about the small things. You say,
please, now, let's not forget things either way.

Market

The produce store but the tomatoes still
aren't good. I say: produce beauty. They lock
up at night behind chicken wire. And will
the city sleep? Darkness about the block
and I get a special kind of sat-is-
fac-tion watching teenagers wipe out on
their bikes, watching the streetlights shake and fizz
on and off again. The graveyard upon
the hill reads to all of us at night, names
father, names mother, names the dearly be
-lovéd. From my seat I look at the frames
on the wall, I look at the dog and see
in his eyes we are thinking the same thing:
red tomatoes, ripe, the gone things dreams bring.

Shaving

Thirty at last and I now find myself
wondering how I got here: heavier
and in love, the dog pacing, a bookshelf
with thousands of words I've forgotten. Sure,
I'm alive and happy, but it is strange
to be an age, strange to be an older
thing getting older. I remember change
was something I wanted. I remember
asking for facial hair, and it came here
to this strange topography of body,
but now I ask it to leave, go back where
you came from, when I was softer, slowly
becoming me, and do I love what is
me, gone, to come, what then, what now, what this.

Mac's Detail Shop

40

Hubcaps, and I see your face reflected.
Convex? Bullshit, son, these rims were shining.
In the parking lot one woman changed
her shirt, the other turned around smiling
at everything you leave when you leave home
for the evening. Streetlights, somewhere the stars
shine, somewhere in a dark garage there's some
guy on his knees with newspaper, three cars
left to detail. We make them pretty. We
make it all so nice. I look at my dash,
and rub the dust off. I look and I see
the dirty cars, the clean cars, the green cash
passing from one hand to another, green
thank you, green please, green Don't that chrome look mean.

Found Sonnet

The dandelions everywhere about
this time of year. And about this we are
never wrong. They are eternal and sprout
always and for ever and I've come far
to tell you a story about a plant
that I think perhaps fancies itself as
something so strong that its singular want,
like that sibyl of somewhere is to pass
on, to exit, to die. The white heads now
explode. I am being dramatic. Roots
root. I sit in the yard and fight, fold, plow,
and with time, hands, curses, and dirty boots
you learn to respect what you can't stop, you
who in windows see the bright, speckled view.

River Running to the Ocean, Ocean Running to the Sea

I wash the gutters, try to patch the house
together with some caulk. I can't say that
without you laughing. That's how words run south
around here. I feel today I want at
least to say something beautiful. The dog
licks his leg and we are alive. Hear me,
then, when I tell you again how the frog
turned into a prince. I think sometimes, see,
that the form of things will take us where it
may, or wants to, or needs to. The rain comes,
off the roof, down the pipes, it spills despite
my pliers, my cursing. That about sums
up the universe, I guess. Random turns
out, and the fairytale ends well (he learns).

Vine

Rusted mailboxes, and the fences keep
cutting the shadows into small diamonds.
I wear a white shirt. It is cool. Down deep
under the ground sometimes a river runs,
old, dark, wet. I suppose there are thousands
of things I know nothing about. Metal
and oxidation, for instance. The winds
as they turn the tulips into several
different directions. Wear can make an old
thing beautiful, it can drop a bridge down
to its knees in the low water, so cold
that it weeps with the ivy, wild and grown
all over everything, the fence, the post,
the brother flowing underground, the lost.

Win, Place, Show

The Kentucky Derby and the 50-
to-1 longshot comes in. I say god bless
the unknown. I was drinking beer, antsy
at an off-track betting joint. I was less
a hundred bucks. I was not a winner.
In the mornings sometimes I think we will
awake and all of our dreams will blister
us with their brightness, surround us, the still
bright hum of everything on our list. This
is too much. The wine glasses run out so
they have to pour the wine into plastic
cups. People do not like this. Some just go
and leave the drink there, trembling. The TVs
flicker. Horses run. I hear the word: please.

Cockscomb the Second

Stakes

Don't know why the train blows so long. Don't know
if the mountains lift me up or knock me
down. Don't know. I take a hoe to the low
rows of the garden. I want veggies, see,
I want tomatoes. They will judge you on
your produce in this lifetime. In the next,
it's not really safe to say. Being gone
sometimes makes you more real. Alone and vexed
to tears. Trouble, I say, I cannot write
a very long sentence. Very well, I
say, the seeds waiting for a bit of light
do not care about this. But still I try
to talk to them, in the low of the rain,
I say this be life, all lovely and pain.

Flash Flood

I say this be life, all lovely and pain.
Things bloom, we talk of children, and behind
all that we both know it'll hurt. Rain, rain,
rain. Everything green and good but the blind
mole has it too easy right now, the seeds
haven't yet had to put up a fight. It's
about seeing what you're made of. Your needs
surrendered, your teeth biting down on bits
of a stick. I holler in the mountains.
I let my shoes off and roll up my pants.
The water keeps rising, and so I sin
against keeping warm and get wet. We dance
around each other between rooms, slowly.
The dog watches birds. Sometimes we're holy.

State Bird

The dog watches birds. Sometimes we're holy
in the low light of morning. The flag up
on the mailbox. I'm trying to slowly
be more quiet. Water rests in the cup
beside the bed, and, looking at the bird
book, you asked me why all the males are more
flashy. It's not like that, I said, but words
weren't right then, the birds weren't drawn right, and sure
there is a difference in color but I
needed to explain the subtlety of
beauty. I'd fail myself right now. And why
does the mockingbird sing what sounds like love
in so many voices? All of those wings.
All those songs in the trees. But still, he sings.

Swing

52

All those songs in the trees. But still, he sings
in the radio, a blue yodel on
the state of heartache. On the porch she brings
me dinner. On the power lines some lone-
some starlings line up and face the sun. You
can't ever explain to someone your child
-hood, or your child, or anything that you
have ever loved. I can't explain the wild,
high-pitched cracking voice moving me to a
deep mix of sorrow and joy inside. Oh,
sing on, sing on. The boot starts tappin'-a-
beat on the floor, the floor starts its long show
of percussion. The heart, too. The leaves swell.
It's spring, by gosh, oh, golly. I am well.

Etymology

It's spring, by gosh, oh, golly. I am well.
9:14, Tuesday, May 5th. They're out there
somewhere biting limes. Where was it we fell
in love, exactly? A seed down from where
it sat on the tree, sits in the ground, grows.
But does it begin there, did it begin
on the tree, did it begin long ago
when that other tree began, did it, in
the greater plan of things, begin written
out in long-hand? Independence Day. Free
me, oh Lord. Chips, salsa, salt on the rim
of a deep green glass. It's a fishbowl, see,
and we're all swimming around. In Spanish:
Via con dios. Translation: I wish.

Transplantation

54

Via con dios. Translation: I wish
I knew exactly. All words are the slight
tears in photographs. The couple in kiss.
The couple torn apart. I sit with white
paper and draw a tree because it is
the only thing I'm good at drawing. And,
darling, you are complete. There's a thing lives
down by the water, burrows in the sand.
Translation: I am afeard of so much.
So, go with god, if there be a god you
know to go with. I go with a small bunch
of flowers in a basket. I go new,
like a babe pulled from the dirt. There is sun.
There are clouds and rain. I take out and run.

Sonnet without End

There are clouds and rain. I take out and run
but I know from the window you are there
watching me. Don't know how I'm given sun.
Don't know why the trains blow so long. You're where
I want to be most in the world. This ain't
a place, babe, but the space that you move in.
Sometimes we're holy. Sometimes we just can't
let loose. You can't ever explain something
you really love. Crocus, then daffodil,
then tulip, then hyacinth. The bulbs come
back every year, and I'm all of them. Still,
they take some water. Still some rain and sun.
Water rests in the cup beside the bed.
Translation: what still grows is never dead.

Sentimental Sonnet

Birds chirp. Lavender blooms, etc.
Maybe people are sick and tired of these
things in poems. Get lost, then. Scram, buster.
Homes, asphalt, homes, asphalt, water, then geese
on the water, lifting out of water
as the first boats roar down the lake. Some days
we feed them bread, the old stuff, and under
the green surface their feet churn. We obey
the weather. Sometimes we let loose and get
out into the rain. No umbrella, yeah,
we roll like that. The storm comes, the small, wet
things get big, poofy on a branch, via
life's circle, head sunk into feathers, a
cheesy old rhyme: rain, sun, plants, song, and us.

Migrating Sonnet

May 7 and independence is stale
by now. We'll walk down to the lake and feed
it to the geese. They're free to go, but, well,
they stay. The water flows west, and the weeds
flower and blow. We're all kind of bound by
a cycle. The time of month when the blood
runs heavy, the time of year when we try
to see the green through the long and dark hood
of thunderstorms. I shake all over now.
If there's a fella holding up the earth,
he's bound, one day, to drop it. And so how
do I arrive as one once pulled from dirt
and water? There's a TV show about
immortality I catch heading out.

Domasticate

The black dog next door opens his big mouth.
Sometimes I get drunk and say too much. We
circle the yard and bark. We head down south
and test the leash. It's that time of the sea
-son where we all get itchy. How come May?
How come that trill at the end of the bird's
song? Chain link. Divvy up the loot, and, hey,
I'll meet you this side of Texas, yessir,
next year. A small tail walks down the street and
everything goes crazy. The wind, the loud
thunder that split my dream last night, and ran
me ragged in two directions. I howled
in one. In the other, I walked the black
road. Fences everywhere. Then I came back.

Doodle-do

Spring rain and the chickens keep quiet. When
the sun comes out and the dogs bark the red
rooster will make his way to the old tin
roof. All I do is sit and fill my head
with coffee and try to appear as if
I'm inconsequential. I don't even
know what I mean by that. I catch a lift
in the back of a pickup. Ain't grievin',
ain't too lazy to crow. Then in sequence
the rooster ruffles up, the dog's neck hair
rises, and I suck in air and flex. Hence,
we're all trying hard to be more than where
we are, the space we occupy, the line
of us expanding: we flare, fire, and shine.

Sugar Tree

Candied pecans at the flea market. Grease
pools in the parking lot puddles. The rain
fills everything up so quickly, and leaves
slowly through the cracks in the earth. The pain
Eliot saw in April I don't at
all times understand. Some days seem to be
eternal. I hold them inside, in that
small little forever bucket. I see
flowers, I am glad. I see you walking
between two rooms, your shadow, and I am
glad. People stand on gravel and keep talking
and smoking cigarettes. At last I can
see the produce getting good. So we'll eat
better, and live forever, and be sweet.

Bi-pass

So I'll open the mailbox and then there
will be your diamond ring. If you're patient
enough the world just comes to you. But where
are you, exactly? Where is the small stent
in my father's heart? We get scared of things
so we try to spend our days building our
confidence. If you look at the bright wings
of the future eventually the hour
comes and everything gets clear. It's all so
real I can't see it sometimes. And will you
marry me? Would you have my baby? Oh,
I'ma die some day but for you, yes, you,
I'ma bloom first. My blood runs. I kind of
get hungry. I believe, foremost, in love.

Cockscomb the Third

Dinner

Mother's Day and we eat some fried chicken.
The buffet steams, and everywhere, people
behave themselves. So we take a lickin'
and keep on tickin'. In the old steeple
the bells ring. It rains. Grass grows. The dog coughs
up something and the worms line the asphalt.
I want to be remembered. I was lost
on the back roads of America, the snot
in my throat, the whisky in the long seat.
They say things are getting better. Today
I believe them. Sunday we get our treat
at the ice cream shop, a sweet cone we pay
for with money from selling our used things.
I miss you when you're gone. Then the phone rings.

Tap

I miss you when you're gone. Then the phone rings
and these people want to test our water.
I tell them no thanks. I'm content, and things
don't bother me much I can't decipher.
We put some grass seed down, and talk a bit
about the mechanics of a yard with
workers at the hardware store. Then we sit
on the porch for a long time, in our filth,
looking out at the neighbor's lawn. She has
bone cancer, and it's hard now to watch her
flowers bloom. I drink water from a glass,
and don't even know her name. I'll never
leave you. I'll be the one who's beside you
in bed. I'll dream of you the whole night through.

Sourwood

In bed, I'll dream of you the whole night through.
You'll wear white, and my hands will be clean, I'll
wash up. The phone rings, and I get up to
see who it is. I believe in the will
and potential of humankind. I want
to be remembered. But more than that I
want to be. All over town people plant
gardens. The old man down the road knows why
bees behave the way they do, sells honey.
We're not so important, after all. But
what's between us, what is, all the money
in the world set to wild fire could not shut
out. I look at the mountains, and hear wind.
The birds chirp and take what food they can find.

Railroad Sonnet

The birds chirp and take what food they can find.
The train whistle blows. I hear the wheels on
the tracks and feel at home. The iron grinds
and moves with the weather. I love a song
about heartache, but not heartache. I'm done
with fiction. Yesterday on the front porch
we put up numbers to mark the house, one
at a time. I know that some use the torch
as a metaphor, but here electric
switches turn and a bulb blows out. Houses
hum all over with worry and the quick
resolve of true love. Women wear blouses
and men, button-downs. We are so pretty
when the morning comes and we get ready.

Landscaping

When the morning comes and we get ready
cars roll by, the buses squeal. I want to
live forever. What say we go steady?
The birds call out for mates, the day is new.
Spring spills all over the place, the lil' babe
can't keep the food in her mouth. Then they pull
a lever and the grain pours, they say Hey
when they need it to stop, and the trucks, full,
drive away. Monday, May 11, and
I'm out of work. I miss you when you're gone.
Someone once asked me if they should use sand
or gravel as a base, when working on
a walkway. I like to dig things up now.
I steal wild plants, and it's good to know how.

Water Heater

I steal wild plants, and it's good to know how
to change a flat, drive a stick, get blood stains
out of khaki pants. 11:20
and I get hungry for lunch. Still it rains.
Showers bring life back, and in the bathroom
I run the water hot. Sometimes I like
to cause myself a bit of pain. The groom
in the dream seemed happy. We took a hike
straight up a mountain and in the distance,
the moonshine stills burned. My father's father
wears a diamond ring. In a football stance
they took my picture once. I am neither
of these legacies, but still I return.
I am yours now. I turn the knob and burn.

Home

I am yours now. I turn the knob and burn
the gravy, just enough. I eat biscuits.
I want to live forever. Yes, we turn
from one year to the next. A small bird hits
the window, and so I wonder if it
ever really saw itself, or, if, once
seeing itself, wanted closer. I drift
back into a dream. June, and there is sun,
you are wearing white, and my hands are clean.
The birds chirp, and take what food they can find.
The spring passes into spring, and the dream
passes into summer. And I don't mind
not knowing so much. Here the flowers bloom.
I push open my heart to make more room.

Sunday Paper

I sit and stare at this check that I need
to cash. 8:29 A.M. and the
economy doesn't really take seed
in my brain this morning. I take all of
the big words and put them in the compost
pile. We wake up and rub each other in
the mornings. The bananas get brown. Most
of all I want to be good for you, sin
no more, etc. In the book you
keep in the bathroom I read about full
-filling your life's purpose. Everyday's new
and that's not always a gift I'm able
to accept. We're in love. I say something
cheesy. Outside at last it stopped raining.

"SHAVING"
ART BY MICAH FARRITOR
THIRTY AT LAST AND I NOW FIND MYSELF
WONDERING HOW I GOT HERE: HEAVIER
AND IN LOVE, THE DOG PACING, A BOOKSHELF
WITH THOUSANDS OF WORDS I'VE FORGOTTEN. SURE,
I'M ALIVE AND HAPPY, BUT IT IS STRANGE
TO BE AN AGE, STRANGE TO BE AN OLDER
THING GETTING OLDER. I REMEMBER CHANGE

WAS SOMETHING I WANTED. I REMEMBER ASKING FOR FACIAL HAIR, AND IT CAME HERE
TO THIS STRANGE TOPOGRAPHY OF BODY,
BUT NOW I ASK IT TO LEAVE, GO BACK WHERE YOU CAME FROM, WHEN I WAS SOFTER, SLOWLY
BECOMING ME, AND DO I LOVE WHAT IS ME, GONE, TO COME, WHAT THEN, WHAT NOW, WHAT THIS.

Shannon Wheeler created Too Much Coffee Man which
has run as a weekly newspaper comic, a web comic, in comic
books, in magazines and collected in graphic novels. Too
Much Coffee Man even lays claim to being the first opera
based on a comic book. *The New Yorker* began publishing
single panel cartoons from Wheeler in 2009. BOOM!
published a collection of New Yorker submissions in the
book *I Thought You Would Be Funnier* (2010). Wheeler is
currently working on a graphic novel about the Gulf Coast
oil spill.

Micah Farritor is an illustrator with okra stuck in his teeth.
He has been working in comics since 2004. His works
include *The Living & The Dead*, *Night Trippers*, the science
fiction comedy series, *White Picket Fences* published by
Ape Entertainment, and "Coyote and the Pebbles" in the
anthology, *Trickster: Native American Tales, A Graphic Collection,*
published by Fulcrum Books. Postcards: True Stories That Never
Happened is by Villard. Micah lives in Wisconsin with his
tireless and forgiving wife, Jodi and his equally tireless and
adorable daughter, Ella.

Clay Matthews is the author of *Superfecta* and two chapbooks: *Muffler* (H_NGM_N B_ _KS) and *Western Reruns* (End & Shelf Books). He currently lives in Johnson City, Tennessee. Visit his blog at claymatthews.blogspot.com.

www.ingramcontent.com/pod-product-compliance
Lightning Source LLC
Chambersburg PA
CBHW032122050726

47590CB00008B/2933